YOU CHOOSE

CAN YOU SURVIVE the 1900 Galveston HURRICANE?

AN INTERACTIVE HISTORY ADVENTURE

by Jessica Gunderson

CAPSTONE PRESS
a capstone imprint

Published by Capstone Press, an imprint of Capstone.
1710 Roe Crest Drive
North Mankato, Minnesota 56003
capstonepub.com

Copyright © 2022 by Capstone. All rights reserved. No part of this publication may be reproduced in whole or in part, or stored in a retrieval system, or transmitted in any form or by any means, electronic, mechanical, photocopying, recording, or otherwise, without written permission of the publisher.

Library of Congress Cataloging-in-Publication Data
Names: Gunderson, Jessica, author.
Title: Can you survive the 1900 Galveston hurricane? : an interactive history adventure / Jessica Gunderson.
Description: North Mankato, Minnesota : Capstone Press, an imprint of Capstone, [2022] | Series: You choose: disasters in history | Includes bibliographical references and index. | Audience: Ages 8-12. | Audience: Grades 4-6.
Summary: "In September 1900, the people of Galveston, Texas, knew a storm was coming. But they'd experienced storms before and didn't think much of it. However, the hurricane that hit on September 8 was more powerful and damaging than anybody expected. Will you find a way to survive the storm and write about the experience for the local newspaper? Can you find a way to save your family's business and the customers inside when the storm hits? Will you rescue a young woman who is floating by on the detached roof of a house in the middle of the storm? With dozens of possible choices, it's up to YOU to find a way to survive through one of the deadliest storms in history"-- Provided by publisher.
Identifiers: LCCN 2021033252 (print) | LCCN 2021033253 (ebook) | ISBN 9781663958938 (hardcover) | ISBN 9781666323504 (paperback) | ISBN 9781666323511 (pdf)
Subjects: LCSH: Galveston (Tex.)--History--20th century--Juvenile literature. | Hurricanes--Texas--Galveston--History--20th century--Juvenile literature. | Floods--Texas--Galveston--History--20th century--Juvenile literature.
Classification: LCC F394.G2 G86 2022 (print) | LCC F394.G2 (ebook) | DDC 976.4/139061--dc23
LC record available at https://lccn.loc.gov/2021033252
LC ebook record available at https://lccn.loc.gov/2021033253

Editorial Credits
Editor: Aaron Sautter; Designer: Bobbie Nuytten; Media Researcher: Morgan Walters; Production Specialist: Laura Manthe

All internet sites appearing in back matter were available and accurate when this book was sent to press.

Printed and bound in China. 5378

TABLE OF CONTENTS

About Your Adventure 5

CHAPTER 1
A Storm Brews............................7

CHAPTER 2
Reporter at the Front 11

CHAPTER 3
A Boy in the Hurricane 43

CHAPTER 4
On Patrol in Galveston....................71

CHAPTER 5
Storm of the Century.....................101

Most Destructive Hurricanes in U.S. History 106
Other Paths to Explore..................... 108
Bibliography............................. 109
Glossary................................. 110
Read More............................... 111
Internet Sites 111
About the Author......................... 112

ABOUT YOUR ADVENTURE

YOU are living in Galveston, Texas, in the year 1900. Thousands of people call Galveston home. The city is well-known as one of the busiest shipping ports in the country.

In September, you hear about a storm heading your way. You've seen storms before and don't think much about it. But when the hurricane hits, it's more powerful than anything you've ever seen. Will YOU make it through the storm alive?

Chapter One sets the scene. Then you choose which path to read. Follow the directions at the bottom of the page as you read the stories. The decisions you make will change your outcome. After you finish one path, go back and read the others for new perspectives and more adventures.

Turn the page to begin your adventure.

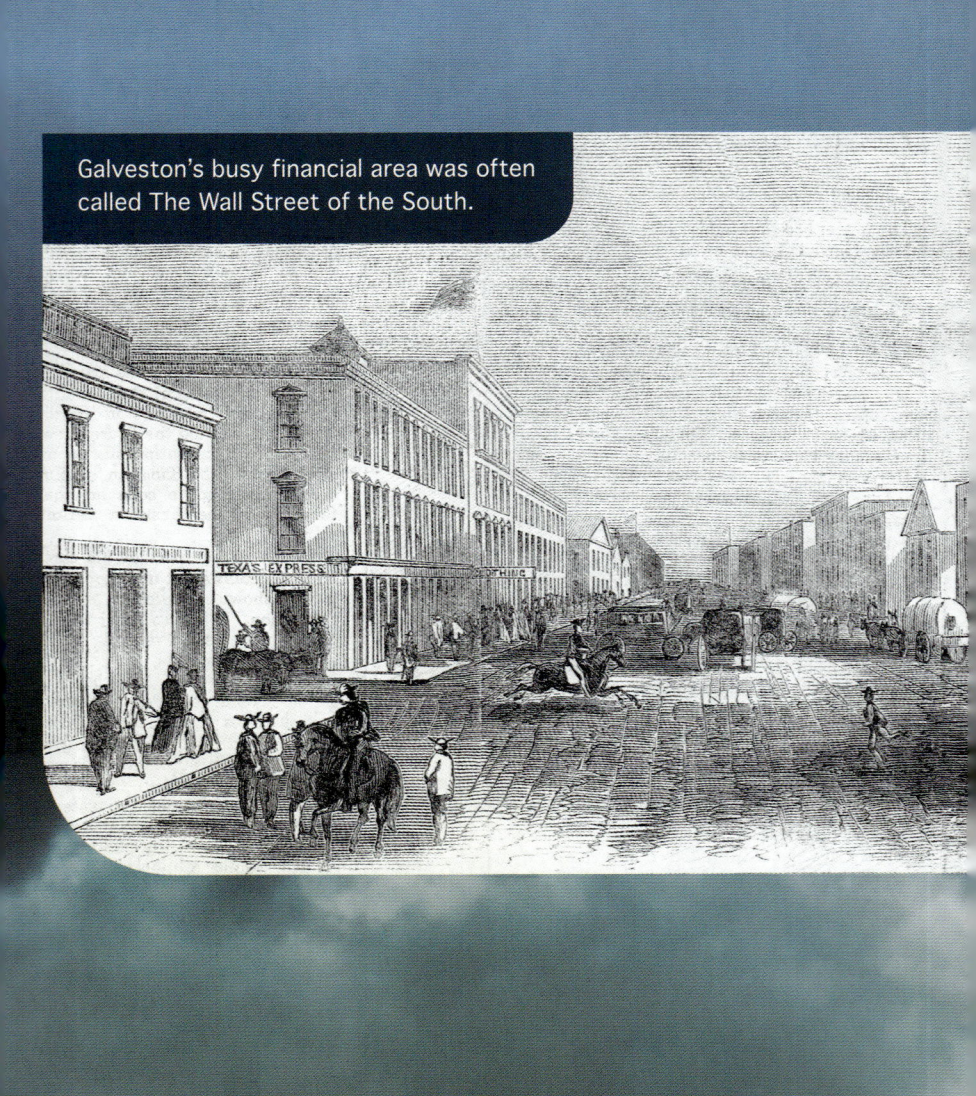

Galveston's busy financial area was often called The Wall Street of the South.

CHAPTER 1
A STORM BREWS

Galveston, Texas, is a city on an island in the Gulf of Mexico. Officially founded in 1839, it became a bustling city with sparkling beaches and a booming waterfront. The Port of Galveston even rivaled New Orleans, Louisiana, as the nation's top exporter of cotton. The Strand financial area was as busy as New York's famous Wall Street financial district.

By 1900 the city had a population of about 38,000 people. Tall, stately mansions lined Broadway, the main street in the city. A causeway linked Galveston to Houston by railroad. Trolley cars traveled along Broadway and the beachfront. Swimmers flocked to the beaches. People cycled and strolled along the boardwalk near the beach.

Turn the page.

However, Galveston had its problems too. Tropical storms often rolled in from the Gulf of Mexico, drenching the city and knocking down trees and small structures. Much of the city was barely above sea level. During storms, the waters of the gulf sometimes rushed in and flooded the low-lying streets and alleyways. Local citizens just called these floods "overflows" and weren't alarmed.

But in 1900 this casual attitude would change. In late August, a tropical cyclone began to form in the Caribbean Sea, and then it swirled into the Gulf of Mexico. The cyclone strengthened and became a hurricane, heading straight toward Galveston.

On September 7, 1900, large swells are forming out in the gulf. The swells crash hard onto Galveston's beachfront. Many residents are gathering on the beach to watch the waves come in.

The swells are dark, swirling with sand lifted from the bottom of the sea. But no one seems concerned. The weather is hot and humid. Everyone is glad that a storm will help cool things down.

Like the other locals, you aren't too alarmed by the coming storm. But by the next day the winds are howling, and the streets are flooding more than ever before. You quickly realize that this isn't any ordinary storm. The situation is dangerous, and many may not live through it.

To cover the storm as a journalist in Galveston, turn to page 11.

To work in your family's restaurant when the storm hits, turn to page 43.

To be a Galveston police officer, turn to page 71.

In the early 1900s, most female journalists worked for a newspaper or magazine's society section. They mainly wrote stories about women's fashion, food, and community events.

CHAPTER 2
REPORTER AT THE FRONT

It's September 8, 1900. You're a young, aspiring journalist on assignment in Houston, Texas. But covering the wedding of a rich couple isn't very exciting, at least not to you.

You've always dreamed of being a reporter who covers exciting stories like wars and disasters. But you're a young woman. Your editor doesn't believe women should cover such stories. Instead, he assigns you to the fashion and society pages.

As the couple take their vows, you scribble descriptions of the bride's dress and the groom's hopeful smile. You know your readers will love all the details you include. But still, you're bored.

Turn the page.

Someone bumps into you, and your pencil goes flying. You almost drop your brand-new Brownie point-and-shoot camera.

"Sorry, miss," says a man, bending down to pick up your pencil. He hands it back to you and looks up at the bright sky above. "I wasn't paying attention. I was watching for the storm."

"Storm?" you ask.

"Haven't you heard?" he says. "A big storm is heading this way." He introduces himself as Peter. "Do you write for the *Houston News* society page?"

"Actually, yes," you beam at the recognition. "I'm working on a story now."

"Sounds like an exciting job," Peter says.

You roll your eyes. "Not really. Nothing exciting ever happens in Houston."

But Peter isn't listening. He's staring up at the clouds again.

"Are you a meteorologist?" you ask.

"Just an amateur," he tells you. "But trust me. This storm is going to be bad! Huge swells are crashing on Galveston's beach. That means the storm is stirring up waves way out in the gulf."

Galveston is just a few miles across the bay from Houston.

Peter leans in close, glancing around him. "I'm heading to Galveston to watch the storm. I can't miss the chance to see this."

If the storm will be as bad as he says, you could land the big story you've always wanted.

"I'm going to Galveston, too," you tell him. "Come on. We can head to the train station together."

Turn the page.

When you reach the train station, it's bustling with people. The train for Galveston is about to depart. At the ticket counter, the station agent tells you there's only one ticket left. But there's another train bound for Galveston, leaving from the town of Beaumont nearby. You could go to Beaumont and catch the train there.

"You can take this train," Peter says. "I'll go on to Beaumont."

You hesitate. Maybe you should go to Beaumont, too, so you can travel together. But you want to get to Galveston soon. You don't want to miss your chance to take photos of the storm.

To take the Beaumont train with Peter, go to page 15.
To take this train, turn to page 18.

The train station is crowded and hot. You would normally be utterly bored, but Peter is entertaining you. He tells you all about his love of weather. In your notebook, he draws various shapes of clouds and labels them.

"Some people think altocumulus clouds are a sign of a hurricane," he tells you. He draws a sketch of a hazy, gray sky.

You're about to look out the window when your train pulls into the station. It's raining, and Peter holds his jacket over your head as you cross the platform onto the train.

At Bolivar Point, the train stops. Here, it will chug aboard a ferry to cross the channel to Galveston. You lean over Peter to peer out the window. Buckets of rain hide your view. Then you see the ferry, fighting its way through huge waves crashing against its bow.

Turn the page.

As the ferry nears the pier, the wind knocks the boat backward. The captain tries to steer the ferry to the pier, but the storm is too strong. The ferry turns back toward Galveston.

"What do we do now?" you cry.

As if in answer, the train starts moving backward. The conductor is taking you back to Beaumont.

"All for nothing," you mutter, staring down at your notebook. Nothing in the notebook is worth anything. Except maybe Peter's sketches.

"It's probably for the best," Peter tells you. Then he gasps and points at the floor.

The train is filling with water—fast.

You look out the window. You don't see land anymore—just water surrounding the entire train.

The train stops. A passenger starts crying. Rain pummels the windows, and the train lurches side to side with the wind.

"Look!" Peter says, pointing out the window. Through the sheets of rain, you see a glimmering light. "It's the Bolivar Point Lighthouse," he says.

"And?" you ask.

"It's not too far. We could make our way there to ride out the storm."

You shiver and look out to see sheets of rain hitting the window. You're not sure going out in this weather is such a good idea. The train rocks again.

To stay on the train, turn to page 20.
To go with Peter to the lighthouse, turn to page 22.

You board the train and wave goodbye to Peter. You wonder if you'll ever see him again.

The train chugs out of Houston and onto the causeway to the island. A fierce wind bucks against the train. Your notebook flies from your hand and skitters into the aisle. Maybe going to Galveston isn't such a good idea after all.

You pick up your notebook and scribble some notes. You describe the slant of the rain outside the window and the vicious roaring of the wind.

Finally, the train pulls up to the station. You look out the window and see that the water is knee-deep. Galveston is already flooding.

The men on the train soon form a human chain. They begin helping women and children across the churning water and into the train station.

Most passengers are heading to the second floor to wait out the storm. Near the entrance, you see a few horse-drawn taxis, called hacks, waiting to take passengers to their destinations.

You came to Galveston for a reason—to capture the storm in photos and writing. You really want to head toward the waterfront. But looking at the swirling flood below, you're not sure the story is worth it anymore. Maybe you should head upstairs with the others.

To go to the second floor, turn to page 24.

To take a hack to the waterfront, turn to page 26.

"I'm not going out in that wind and rain," you tell Peter. "The train is the safest place." Seeing Peter's concerned look, you add, "I'm sure this storm will blow over soon anyway."

He shakes his head. "I hope so, too," he says.

Peter and a handful of others step off the train. You wipe moisture from the window and look out. But you don't see anyone outside, just whirling rain.

Then, miraculously, the train begins moving again. You sit back in your seat, confident you've made the right decision.

But the train only makes it a few miles. A huge wave crashes over the top of the train. You hold onto your seat as the train car topples over. You slide off your seat and slam into the side of the train. Dazed, you look up at the windows. Rising waters cover the entire train.

The storm's fierce winds and floodwaters derailed and destroyed many of Galveston's train cars and tracks.

Days later, rescue crews find the train buried in sand and debris. You and the other 84 passengers are all dead.

THE END

To follow another path, turn to page 9.
To learn more about the hurricane, turn to page 101.

You cling to Peter's hand as you step off the train. A few others have joined you. You form a chain with each person holding another's hand.

The water is waist-high. But the lighthouse isn't far. You and the others make your way slowly across the flooded ground.

The light beckons like a beacon in the storm. As you reach the doorway of the lighthouse, you glance back at the train. You can barely see it through the storm, but you think you see a puff of steam. The train is moving again.

Inside the lighthouse, nearly 200 people are gathered. They sit on the spiral staircase that rises through the middle of the tower.

You keep clinging to Peter's hand and never let go through the long night. As water seeps into the building, you and the others move higher up the spiral stairs.

Thankfully, the lighthouse is strong enough to withstand the storm. You, Peter, and everyone inside survive. But 85 passengers who stayed on the train weren't so lucky. They died when the hurricane washed the train away.

THE END

To follow another path, turn to page 9.
To learn more about the hurricane, turn to page 101.

You mount the stairs to the second floor. Dozens of stranded passengers are crowded together near the stairs. You squeeze in next to them. Even though there's tension in the air, you can't help but feel a little bored. The most excitement you had was wading through the water to the station.

Then a woman screams and points toward the stairs. You crane your neck to get a better look. Water is slowly creeping up the stairs. But that's not all you see—a body is floating up in the water, too.

It's time to get out of here, you realize. Soon even the second floor might be completely flooded. And more dead bodies might come with it.

Broadway is the highest street in the city. Huge mansions line the street, and you've covered many stories of high society parties there. Someone is certain to recognize you and give you shelter.

You take the back staircase and slosh through water on the main floor of the train station. As you step outside, a fierce wind and bullets of rain pelt your head. You stuff your notebook deep inside your dress pocket so it doesn't get wet.

Others have the same idea as you. You see people carrying children, suitcases, boxes, and blankets. One woman is even lugging a table lamp.

The wind is carrying dangerous objects too. Broken shingles and pieces of roofs fly through the air. You duck your head to avoid being struck.

Up ahead, you see a horse-drawn cart. The cart is empty, and the horse is standing with its head down, getting pelted by the rain.

You might be able to get to Broadway more quickly if you take the cart. It isn't yours, but there's no sign of the owner anywhere.

To take the cart, turn to page 36.
To keep going on foot, turn to page 38.

You splash toward the closest hack and climb in. "To the beach," you tell the driver.

"I wouldn't if I were you, miss," the driver says.

You fish in your bag for some coins and drop them in the driver's hands. "I'm a reporter," you say, showing him your camera bag.

He shakes his head. "I'll take you as close as I can," he says. "But the streets are already flooding. And this storm is about to become a hurricane. I can feel it!"

A hurricane! Even better, you think, patting your camera. "I just need to take some photos of the storm," you say. "I'll bet no other reporter is brave enough to do so!"

He shakes his head and snaps the reins. "Wouldn't quite call it bravery," he mutters.

He drives up close to the waterfront and lets you out. Water whooshes around your feet.

The beach is no longer a beach at all. The Gulf's waters have risen over the sand. The bath house has tipped over and bobs in the waves. The gulf roars, as tall waves churn and crash.

You don't see anyone else on the beach. You take some photos, knowing you'll be the only person to get such great shots.

But the storm is getting worse. You're putting yourself in danger, just for a chance to be famous.

Suddenly you see you're not alone. A dark figure comes toward you. He's yelling something you can't quite hear. Then he stops and waves both his arms, beckoning you to follow.

To ignore the man and take a few more photographs, turn to page 28.

To follow the man, turn to page 30.

You wade along the beach, snapping photos. The sky grows dark, even though it's the middle of the afternoon. You wonder if the pictures will turn out with the dim lighting.

Suddenly, a strong wave knocks you over. You struggle to stand, but the water pulls you down again. Something knocks into you, and you realize it's part of a roof of someone's house. You climb onto the roof and cling to the sides.

Soon you can't see anything at all. The roof swirls as the rain pummels you.

You hang on tight as you float for hours. The rain drenches you, and you've never been so cold in your life.

In the middle of the night, the moon peeks through the clouds. The storm is fading. That's the good news. The bad news is that you're floating in the gulf, far away from Galveston.

You doubt there's any chance of rescue out here.

But in the morning, you catch a glimpse of land. The tide pulls you toward it. Stunned, you realize it's the city of Galveston. When you stumble onto shore, you can't believe there's almost nothing left of the city. Only a few buildings remain standing.

Luckily, you are alive and well. But the same can't be said about your camera. It lies somewhere on the bottom of the Gulf of Mexico. The photographs you risked your life to get will never see the light of day.

THE END

To follow another path, turn to page 9.
To learn more about the hurricane, turn to page 101.

Waves grip your feet, and you know it's time to get off the beach. You make your way to the man, and he grabs your arm, pulling you along with him. You get a glimpse of his face. It's Isaac Cline, Galveston's meteorologist.

You sigh with relief. He'll know what to do.

"It's turning into a hurricane!" he yells, pointing at the swirling clouds above.

"I've got some great photographs!" you yell back, tapping your camera case.

He nods, and you both stumble away from the roaring waves, making your way to Isaac's house. He promises you'll be safe there.

Isaac leads you to a room where his family and some friends are gathered. You sit on the floor next to a young woman. She tells you that her husband left their house to get supplies. He never returned, so she came to the Clines' home.

Others start sharing their stories too. You take mental notes of what they tell you, knowing each story will make a great news article to pair with your photographs.

In one corner of the room, Isaac stands with his brother, Joseph. Their voices rise in anger over the battering wind outside. "We need to move to the center of the city," Joseph says.

"The house is sturdy!" Isaac cries. "And we'd all be killed out there."

"Can't you hear the wind?" Joseph yells. "This house will not stand!"

You jot down the conversation in your notebook. You feel shaken by the argument. *Is Joseph right?* you wonder. Soon you get your answer.

Turn the page.

CRASH!

Something strikes the house and it slides off its foundation. The house is breaking apart and folding into itself. Books, tables, lamps, and glass rain down on you as you swirl into the wreckage.

You lose consciousness for a moment. When you open your eyes, you see Isaac and his family clinging to a broken piece of roof. You could swim toward them, but you don't know if the roof will hold you too.

To swim toward the Clines, go to page 33.

To find something else to use as a raft, turn to page 34.

"Over here!" you cry, bobbing up and down in the water.

But Isaac can't hear you above the wind. He holds his six-year-old daughter close.

You kick your legs, moving slowly toward them. But your skirt bogs you down. You rip your skirt apart with one hand while paddling with the other.

Unfortunately, your water-soaked clothing is too heavy. It pulls you beneath the waves, even though you kick your legs frantically.

Your last thought is that at least you got a good story. Even if you didn't live long enough to write it.

THE END

To follow another path, turn to page 9.
To learn more about the hurricane, turn to page 101.

Something else is bobbing in the waves. Its shape is tall and boxy. At first you think it's the house. Then you realize it's just the porch. It was ripped from the rest of the house by the storm. Pillars still connect the porch with its roof.

The porch would make a great raft. You swim toward it and grip one of its pillars to pull yourself up. You hold on for dear life as the hurricane whips the water into a frenzy. Your arms ache from holding onto the pillar, but you don't give up. Hours later when the storm weakens, you sprawl across the porch floor and fall asleep.

You survived the hurricane, but your work isn't done. You have a story to write. Surprisingly, your camera is still intact, and the film inside wasn't ruined. You later write a detailed story about the hurricane, the people you met along the way, and how you survived. Your story receives national honors.

The deadly hurricane's destruction of Galveston, Texas, made front-page news across the country.

Your editor offers you a promotion, but you decline. Instead, you set off on a trip across the United States. You hope to have enough adventures to write a book someday.

Maybe you'll even run into Peter, the amateur weatherman. You just hope to never encounter another hurricane ever again.

THE END

To follow another path, turn to page 9.
To learn more about the hurricane, turn to page 101.

You hop onto the cart and take the reins. But the horse doesn't budge.

You snap the reins once, and then again. Finally, the horse bucks and takes off. He's just as wild as the storm, twisting through the flooded streets. As he takes a sharp turn, the reins fly from your slippery hands, and you have no control over the horse.

City streets were filled with the wreckage of destroyed buildings after the storm.

As you slide around on the cart seat, you suddenly hear a *THUNK*! Then a *SPLASH*! Something has fallen from the cart.

You look down and see that your camera is gone! You can't leave your Brownie behind.

As you lean over the side of the cart to look for your camera, the horse takes another sharp turn, and you tumble out of the cart.

The water is deeper than you expected. What used to be a street is now a river, and a strong current whisks you away. You become just one of the thousands who drown in the Galveston hurricane.

THE END

To follow another path, turn to page 9.
To learn more about the hurricane, turn to page 101.

The wind batters you as you make your way toward Broadway. The bottom of your skirt is soaked and weighs you down.

Up ahead, you see Broadway and the row of towering stone mansions. The Walker mansion is the closest. You attended a party there a few months ago, and you wrote a great story about it. You hope the Walkers remember you.

You pound on the door, and a servant opens it. When she sees your messy appearance, she begins to slam the door in your face. But then Mrs. Walker appears at her shoulder. She peers at you as you shout your name.

"Ah, yes," she says. "You're the fiery young reporter from Houston. Please come in."

Water puddles at your feet as you step inside. You're about to apologize when you realize that the entire floor is soaked.

"Come upstairs," Mrs. Walker says. You follow her up the stairs, where a dozen people are gathered in the hallway. Someone hands you a piece of bread. You scarf it down, realizing how hungry you were.

Wind hammers the windows of the bedrooms around you.

WHAM! A door slams.

CRASH! You hear glass breaking.

You think about Peter and realize he was right. The storm is unlike any Galveston has seen before! Even this brick mansion is getting battered. A sense of worry sets over the group.

Then someone starts singing. At first, you think it's ridiculous to sing songs when the city is crashing down around you. But when you join in, you realize it helps to calm your nerves.

Turn the page.

You keep singing even as more windows break and water seeps into the hallway. You keep singing even as you shiver with cold.

After several hours, the storm weakens, and the wind stops howling so fiercely. You've made it through the hurricane.

But not all of Galveston is so lucky. The hurricane has flattened thousands of buildings in the city. More than 8,000 people are dead or missing.

In the bright morning sun, you pick your way through the rubble, helping people search for their loved ones. As you do, you listen to their stories. You talk to many women who have lost husbands, parents, and children.

In the coming months, you take the Women's Pages of the Houston newspaper in a new direction. Each week, you write a story of one of Galveston's female survivors. Before long, you become well-known for your touching stories about one of the biggest storms in history.

THE END

To follow another path, turn to page 9.
To learn more about the hurricane, turn to page 101.

While still far out at sea, hurricanes can churn up large, powerful waves that crash on shore.

CHAPTER 3
A BOY IN THE HURRICANE

Saturdays should be fun for a boy of 14. But not for you. Saturday is your day to work at your family's restaurant in downtown Galveston.

But you don't mind. You love the restaurant. Ever since your father died, it's been your duty to help keep it running. Your mother is busy taking care of your younger sister and brothers.

Today you arrive at the restaurant feeling groggy. Yesterday after school you went with your friends to the beach to watch the huge swells come in. The swells mean a storm is brewing out in the Gulf of Mexico. A storm will probably hit Galveston today. But that's nothing new here.

Turn the page.

When you get to the restaurant, you head to the kitchen to say hello to the cook. But he's not there. Instead, you find a note. The cook is staying home today because of the coming storm.

You sigh. You'll be even busier than usual, taking orders *and* doing the cooking. But that's okay. You love to cook. You always add a secret spice to the popular beef sandwiches.

As the first customers trickle in, you recognize Ralph, Sam, and Leonard. They're businessmen who work on Broadway. They always come in for Saturday lunch.

Ralph takes a bite of the sandwich you place in front of him. "*Mmm*, better than usual!" he says.

"That's because I'm cooking today," you say proudly. "The cook stayed home because of the storm."

Leonard chortles. "Storm?" he asks. "It's just a bit of rain."

"Besides," Sam adds, "Isaac Cline, the weatherman, says nothing can destroy Galveston!"

The door swings open, and a rush of wind rustles the menus. The new customers are dripping wet and laughing.

More and more customers keep coming in. You're so busy cooking and serving that you barely notice the wind screaming outside the windows. When you finally have a free minute, you peek outside.

The sidewalk and street are flooded. You begin to worry. Overflow is not unusual during storms, but the flooding could get worse. Maybe you should close the restaurant and head home to check on your family.

Turn the page.

Downtown Galveston was home to many churches, restaurants, and stores.

But the restaurant is crowded. If you close, you'll lose all the money the restaurant makes at lunch. And it's not even noon yet.

To close the restaurant, go to page 47.
To stay open, turn to page 49.

You tell the customers they need to head home. Many start grumbling as they stand up.

"It's for your own safety," you tell them. "So you can get home before the storm gets worse."

"I might not ever come back," Ralph warns.

You give him a smile. "Of course you will! You love my beef sandwiches."

You're drenched by the time you get home. Your feet squish in your wet shoes. Your home is in chaos. Your sister is splashing in puddles in the yard while your little brothers are inside crying. You find your mother hauling things upstairs. Her arms are full of books and photographs.

She barely glances at you. "Help me carry this stuff upstairs," she says, heading for the steps. Your three-year-old brother clings to her legs, not letting her go.

Turn the page.

As you head for the kitchen to gather items, you have an idea. You remember reading that cutting holes in the floor can keep a flooded house on its foundation. The holes fill with water, which eases the water pressure and helps keep the house stable.

It's worth a try, you think. You grab an axe and lift it high over your head.

"Stop! What on earth are you doing?" your mother shouts.

You explain the theory, and she shakes her head. "That's ridiculous. I don't believe it," she says. "Help me instead."

> To keep chopping holes, turn to page 51.
> To help your mother carry belongings, turn to page 53.

You keep cooking, serving, and chatting with your customers. The sky outside darkens, and you light some kerosene lamps to brighten the room.

As you move through the dining room, you step in a puddle of water. You dip your finger in the water and put it to your lips. Salt. It's not just rainwater—it's seawater from the gulf.

You think fast. Upstairs is a printing business. Since it's Saturday, the business isn't open. There will be plenty of room up there for you and your customers.

"Attention, everyone!" you call.

The customers stop talking and look at you. You put on your charming grin. "The building is starting to flood," you tell them. "Grab your sandwiches, and head up to the second floor!"

Turn the page.

No one makes a move.

"I'm comfortable here," Ralph says.

"Yeah," another customer agrees. "I'm not moving!"

"I'll go," says Sam. He stands and picks up his sandwich.

A few others stand, but most customers remain seated. Some of them start grumbling under their breath.

You don't want to make your customers unhappy. What if they never come back? *A little water never hurt anyone,* you tell yourself. But still, you'd like to get upstairs, away from the water.

> To go upstairs, turn to page 56.
> To stay in the restaurant, turn to page 64.

You explain again to your mother why chopping holes will work. "The water will have someplace to go," you say, "It'll fill the holes and hold the house in place rather than push it over."

She grabs a couple loaves of bread from the pantry. "I still don't believe it. But do what you like," she says. "These floors will be ruined anyway." She nods toward the front door, and you see that water is already seeping in.

You chop holes in the kitchen, living room, and dining room floors. Then you head upstairs. Your mother is in her bedroom with the younger kids. Outside, the wind howls and batters the house.

When your siblings are asleep, you creep out in the hall and look downstairs. The first floor is completely flooded. The front door has blown off its hinges, and water is creeping up the stairs. You hurry back to the bedroom.

Turn the page.

CRASH! The sound comes from above you. Your mother screams and points. Above you, the roof is lifting off the house and crashing back down again. It feels like the house could soon collapse.

The kids wake up and begin to howl. You catch your mother's eye. You know she's afraid, but she begins to sing. Behind her, out the window, you see glowing lights.

Your neighbor's house is standing solid. Lamps glow in the windows. You know they'll welcome your family. However, the water is too deep to wade in, and your little brothers can't swim. But you can. Everyone could pile onto a mattress, and you could swim them across.

Or you could stay in the house and hope you survive.

> To use the mattress as a raft, turn to page 58.
> To stay in the house, turn to page 59.

You put the axe down and grab a box instead. You fill it with photographs and silverware and take it upstairs. As you pass your mother, she smiles at you. "Thank you," she says. "I knew you would help."

You make trip after trip up the stairs, grabbing everything you can carry. On your final trip, you grab bread and meat from the kitchen and a kerosene lamp.

Upstairs, your mother is sitting on her bed with your siblings. You join them, knowing it will be a long night. You light the lamp and open a book of fairy tales.

"Once upon a time," you begin.

Outside, the storm roars. The wind is so strong, the whole house seems to move.

Turn the page.

No, not seems to, you realize. *It is moving.*

As the house slides, the lamp rolls to the floor and smashes. The room is in utter darkness now. You reach for your siblings' hands. "Hold on to each other!" you cry.

The wind howls again, and this time you hear splintering wood. Rain rushes at your face.

The house is collapsing.

"We should leave," you tell your mother as calmly as possible.

A flash of lightning reveals her face. Her mouth is grim. "I'm staying," she says.

Another blast of wind crashes against the house. Any minute, the ceiling could fall on you and the kids.

The hurricane's powerful winds toppled many homes and buildings off their foundations.

You could feel your way across the room to the window. But it might not be any safer out there either. And you don't want to leave your mother.

Turn to page 62.

"Follow me," you say to Sam and the other customers willing to go upstairs. You lead them to the back hall and up a flight of stairs.

Upstairs, you and the others plop down on the floor among stacks of paper and gigantic printing presses. Suddenly, you feel the floor beneath you move. Wind pounds at the walls. Maybe you're not safe up here either.

Suddenly, you hear a giant *CRACK!* The next thing you know, you're lying on the floor of your restaurant. You sit up, dazed. Sam is next to you, looking dazed too.

You look around and realize the second floor collapsed. The giant printing press has smashed several tables to splinters. Sadly, some of your customers on the first floor were killed.

You hear someone moaning. It's Ralph. He's covered in blood.

"He needs a doctor!" Sam cries, staggering to his feet.

A few more moans erupt from around the room. Ralph isn't the only one who needs a doctor.

You volunteer to fetch the doctor. You grab a large pasta pot to cover your head. Then you head out into the storm. Wind and rain pummel you as you make your way through the flooded streets.

"Help!" you hear. You see a young man flailing in the water. As you get closer, you see that the rushing water is swirling around a drainpipe. He's being sucked under.

You're unsure what to do. If you stop and help him, you could both drown. And your customers need a doctor fast.

To help the young man, turn to page 66.
To go get the doctor, turn to page 68.

Your mother agrees with the plan. Together you hoist the mattress from the bed. Then you slide it down the stairs and let it rest on top of the water. Your mother lifts your sister and brothers onto the mattress one by one.

"Where are we going?" your youngest brother whimpers. His eyes are wide and watery.

"A boat ride!" you say. You get a good grip on the mattress and push it out the door.

Unfortunately, you're no match for the storm. As you push through the water, you lose your grip on the mattress and go under. You beat your legs and arms against the raging current, but you never surface. As you swirl into the darkness, you just hope that your family makes it to the neighbor's house alive.

THE END

To follow another path, turn to page 9.
To learn more about the hurricane, turn to page 101.

The roof lifts and slams down again. "Maybe we should move to the hallway," your mom suggests. "The center of the house might be the best."

She's right. The hallway has no windows. You huddle there with your family. The roof lifts and slams against the house over and over. Glass shatters as the windowpanes break. The minutes feel like hours. Finally, the wind lessens. The hurricane has passed, and your house is still standing. You and your family have survived.

In the morning, you go outside to investigate. The destruction is unreal. Only a handful of buildings remain standing.

You pick your way through the debris toward the restaurant. Nothing looks the same. To your horror, the restaurant is gone, swept away by the storm. You don't know how your family will survive.

Turn the page.

You head home, climbing over huge piles of broken roofs, walls, and furniture. You try not to look at the dead bodies among the wreckage.

When you tell your mother about the restaurant, she hangs her head. You pat her shoulder. "At least we're alive," you say. You don't want to tell her about all the dead bodies you saw, but she'll find out soon enough.

Over the next few weeks, you volunteer to help clean up the city. So much has been destroyed, you don't know how the city will be rebuilt.

The Red Cross brings water and food to Galveston. You manage to get some beef and bread. One day you surprise your fellow volunteers with your famous beef sandwiches.

"Wow!" one of the workers says after taking a bite. "This sandwich is amazing! You should open a restaurant!"

It took many years to clean up and rebuild Galveston after the hurricane destroyed most of the city.

You look around at the rubble, imagining what the city will look like when it's rebuilt. Your eyes fill with tears.

"That's my plan," you say, smiling through the tears.

THE END

To follow another path, turn to page 9.
To learn more about the hurricane, turn to page 101.

"I'm not leaving you," you tell your mother. You huddle together with the kids in between you.

Above you the roof starts to break apart. Something hits you hard on the head, and you're out cold.

Sometime later you wake up. You're all alone, floating on what used to be the bedroom floor. "Mother!" you call. "Anyone?"

No one answers. Sheets of rain drench you. Your hands are so cold, you don't know how you can hang on to the floor, which is now your raft.

You cling to the makeshift raft as it swivels through the water. You have no idea where you are, but you sense you've traveled far. You hope the storm doesn't take you out into the gulf.

Suddenly the wind shifts. The raft smacks into a pile of rubble. The rubble seems sturdier than the raft.

You scramble onto the rubble pile, clinging to it as it swirls through the floodwater. Sometime in the middle of the night, the storm passes, and the moon peeks through the clouds.

When it is light, you climb down from the pile of rubble. The city around you has been destroyed. You meet some survivors who tell you that people are gathering at the courthouse to find loved ones. Under the bright sun, you make your way through the destroyed city.

On the courthouse steps, you see a familiar shape. It's your little sister! You hug and cry. Your mother and brothers soon appear too. Somehow you all made it through the storm alive.

THE END

To follow another path, turn to page 9.
To learn more about the hurricane, turn to page 101.

You smile at Ralph and Leonard. "I'll stay down here then," you say. Sam shakes his head and makes his way to the stairs.

Ralph nods at you. "Good," he says. He gestures at his sandwich. "I just might order another one of these."

"Got any jokes?" Leonard asks. "That might keep people happy while the storm rages."

Outside, the wind beats against the building and the walls shake. You raise your voice over the noise.

"I certainly do have some jokes! What has ears but can't hear?" you ask, grinning at your customers.

They smile back at you, waiting for the punch line.

But it never comes. The wind gives the building another shake. You hear a terrible creaking and groaning noise overhead. Then you hear a loud CRACK! and look up just as the second floor collapses. A giant printing press falls from above and crushes you instantly.

THE END

To follow another path, turn to page 9.
To learn more about the hurricane, turn to page 101.

"Help!" the man calls again. You know you can't leave the man to die.

You look around quickly. A long plank of wood is lodged against a nearby tree. You can hold on to the tree with one hand and hold out the plank with the other. Hopefully it will be long enough for the man to grab.

People can drown easily in a storm's swirling floodwaters.

You wrap one arm around a low tree branch and stretch the wooden plank out toward the man. His fingers close around the plank, and you pull as hard as you can. Finally, the man breaks free of the whirlpool's grasp.

"Thank you," he gasps.

You drop the plank and let go of the tree. But that's a big mistake. The whirling water sucks you in, and you swirl toward the drain. Water closes over you, and everything goes dark.

At least you helped save someone, even though it cost you your life.

THE END

To follow another path, turn to page 9.
To learn more about the hurricane, turn to page 101.

You struggle into the wind toward the doctor's office, but it keeps pushing you back. Flying objects ping against the pot on your head.

Sadly, you realize there's no way you'll make it to the doctor in time. You need to find shelter fast.

You crouch next to a tree, holding to its trunk as the wind pushes against you. Then you hear shouts. A small boat is gliding down the flooded street.

"Here! Over here!" you shout into the wind. The boat veers toward you, and two boys about your age pull you aboard.

"We're out rescuing people," one boy tells you. "We're taking them to the school on 10th Street."

"I'd like to help," you offer. "But just one thing. I have a restaurant filled with customers that I'd like to save first."

Through the long night, you row through Galveston. You battle through wind and rain, pulling people from the water or under debris. When morning comes, dozens are alive because of you and the other boys.

THE END

To follow another path, turn to page 9.
To learn more about the hurricane, turn to page 101.

In the 1800s and early 1900s, police officers often drove horse-drawn patrol wagons.

CHAPTER 4
ON PATROL IN GALVESTON

It is September 8, 1900. You're heading to the police station at City Hall to report for police duty. A storm is coming, and rain is already falling hard. By the time you reach City Hall, the streets of Galveston are starting to flood.

Chief Ketchum is sitting at his desk, looking exhausted already. "Reporting for duty, sir," you say.

"We need you to make some rescues," he says. "Take the patrol wagon to Lucas Terrace. Residents there are worried about the rising water. Bring them to City Hall."

"Yes, sir," you agree.

Turn the page.

Lucas Terrace is a large apartment building near Galveston Beach. You don't like the idea of going out in the storm, but it's part of the job.

"None of the taxis are willing to go that far east," Ketchum adds. "It's up to us to get the residents out. We've made a couple of trips already."

You nod and head out to the patrol wagon. You jump on to the horse-drawn cart, steady your hat against the wind, and slap the reins. As you move east, the water gets deeper. The wagon slides side to side in the flood, but the horses barrel on.

You get as close as you can to the building and tie the horses to a tree. Then you wade through the floodwater to the entrance. Inside, the floors are only slightly wet, and the building seems solid.

You walk through the hallways pounding on doors. No one answers. You wonder if everyone has evacuated already. On the second floor, a door swings open at your knock.

A woman introduces herself as Mrs. McGillis. "We're fine here," she says. "We aren't going out in this! But won't you come in? Some cookies are just coming out of the oven."

The powerful storm reduced the Lucas Terrace apartment buildings to a pile of rubble.

Turn the page.

"I need to keep making rounds," you tell her. But the smell of chocolate drifts from the apartment.

Just one cookie won't hurt, you think.

Mrs. McGillis's husband appears at her shoulder. "I'm afraid you won't make it very far now," he says, gesturing at the window, which is dark with rain. "What good will it do? You might as well stay here and wait out the storm. I'm sure it will blow by soon. You can make your rounds then."

Mr. McGillis might be right. You probably won't get anywhere if you go back out.

But then again, you made an oath to protect and serve the city.

To take shelter with the McGillis family, go to page 75.

To keep making rounds, turn to page 78.

You step inside the apartment. "I'll stay for a bit, just until the storm breaks," you say. You follow the McGillises into the living room. Several other people are already sitting on the furniture and the floor.

"We offered shelter to anybody who needs it," Mrs. McGillis tells you. "And Lucas Terrace is the sturdiest building in the area."

You take a seat across from a window so you can keep an eye on the storm. Mrs. McGillis hands you a few cookies.

One of the guests reads some comforting verses from the Bible. Then another guest begins to sing and others join in. Soon you're belting out a tune with the rest. When the song is over, you hear a *THUD!* below you. Then another. The sound is coming from the floor below. The guests hear the sounds too and hush.

Turn the page.

"What is that?" a frightened woman asks.

You run to the window and look out. Water has surrounded the building. Your theory on the noise is right.

"The first floor is flooded," you say. "The furniture is knocking against the ceiling below."

"If the first floor is flooded," says one man, "then this building won't be stable for long."

As he finishes speaking, the floor beneath you lurches. You're nearly knocked off balance. Then you hear a terrible crash, followed by chunks of plaster falling from the ceiling.

Mr. McGillis grabs your arm. "You have to see this!" he says.

You follow him into the dining room, and he points out the window. You're looking directly into another window. Several faces stare back at you. One person waves.

"That's the other wing of the building. It looks sturdier than ours," Mr. McGillis tells you. He holds up an ironing board just as the chandelier behind you falls and shatters on the floor. "We could use this to crawl across."

"That's a good idea," you say. Then you hesitate. You don't want anyone to know that you're afraid of heights. And it's a long way down to the churning water below.

To crawl into the other wing of the building, turn to page 80.

To stay in the McGillis apartment, turn to page 83.

You tip your hat to Mrs. McGillis. "Thank you kindly," you say. "But I'd best make my rounds."

Mr. and Mrs. McGillis grimly wish you luck and shut the door.

You continue knocking on doors, but no one is willing to leave with you. You'll have to return to City Hall alone.

Outside, the water is deeper than your knees as you struggle toward the police wagon. Luckily, it hasn't been washed away. The horses stand calmly against the tree.

The water has risen steadily, and the wagon feels like a boat spinning through the streets. You keep an eye out for people who might need help. Up ahead, you see a woman pushing through the driving rain toward the beach. You don't know why she's not heading toward higher ground. You halt the wagon next to her.

The woman clambers into the wagon. "I'll take you to City Hall. You'll be safe there," you tell her.

"No!" she shouts. "I need to find my husband. He's in his office." She points in the direction of the rising water. "Please help him!"

You snap the reins and steer the wagon east toward the beach. Up ahead, you see swirling water. The road is completely washed out.

"We can't go any further," you tell the woman.

"If you can't help me," she says accusingly, "then I'll just get out and walk." She stands up to get off the wagon.

"Wait!" you shout.

You look doubtfully at the pool of water. Your horses have been reliable so far. Maybe you could make it.

To plunge through the water, turn to page 94.
To turn back, turn to page 95.

You and Mr. McGillis slide the ironing board across to the opposite window. The residents there hold it steady.

One by one, you and Mr. McGillis help others onto the board. The wind and rain batter them as they crawl across. You try not to look, in case you lose your nerve.

"Ready?" you ask Mr. McGillis.

He tells you to go first, but you insist he go. You're a police officer, after all. It's your duty to help others.

Mr. McGillis makes it across, and then it's your turn. You hope the ironing board holds steady. Bit by bit, you crawl across. A strong gust of wind grabs your hat and tosses it into the air. Below you, the water rages.

Finally, Mr. McGillis pulls you through the window. You conquered your fear, and you're safe for now.

The apartment is packed with a dozen stranded people. "The bathroom and the bedroom are the safest rooms," Mr. McGillis tells you.

To shelter in the bedroom, turn to page 84.
To shelter in the bathroom, turn to page 86.

After the storm, the people of Galveston had to dig through huge piles of mud and debris to recover the bodies of storm victims.

You hold the ironing board steady as Mr. McGillis helps usher each of the stranded guests through the window.

Then it's Mr. McGillis's turn. "You should go across, officer," he says.

You shake your head. "I'll stay here and hold down the fort," you say with a smile. Mr. McGillis shrugs and bids you well. Then he disappears out the window.

You crouch in the hallway. The building rocks back and forth in the wind. Then the wind seems to stop. Wondering if the storm is over, you go to a window to look outside. Just then, the window explodes! The blast sucks you out through the window and to your certain death.

THE END

To follow another path, turn to page 9.
To learn more about the hurricane, turn to page 101.

You find a spot in the bedroom. Outside, waves crash against the window. The flood has reached the second floor.

CRASH!

A loud crash startles everybody. The other wing of the building, where the McGillis apartment was, is collapsing into the floodwaters! Bricks sail through the bedroom window, smashing the windowpane. You grab blankets and pillows from the bed.

"Protect your heads!" you call and toss them to the crowd.

The minutes drag into hours. No one sings. A few people pray. Finally, the storm lessens. You stand and look out the window. You realize this room is the only thing left standing. The rest of the building has been washed away.

As the morning sun rises, you feel as though you're in a nightmare. Nothing is left of the city except a few buildings. Piles of debris and bodies are everywhere.

You can't believe you survived.

But the chief isn't pleased with you. You didn't follow his orders. He decides to give you a gruesome task. There are too many dead to be buried on land, so the bodies must be hauled out to sea. And you'll be doing the hauling.

Turn to page 96.

In the bathroom, you crouch in the clawfoot tub. Soon you realize the bathroom isn't the safest place to be. The outside wall shakes with the force of the wind. Then the wall blows apart.

You hold tight to the lip of the bathtub as it slides across the floor and out into the flood. For a while, the tub floats. But it starts filling with water, and soon it might sink. You need to find another raft.

As lightning flashes around you, you weigh your options. Pieces of debris swirl in the water. You see a large section of roof several feet away. It seems sturdy, but you'll have to swim toward it.

Closer to you are several window shutters that are tied together. The shutters must have been someone else's makeshift raft. But whoever used it is no longer on it. Not a good sign.

> To jump to the makeshift raft, go to page 87.
> To swim to the roof, turn to page 88.

You launch yourself onto the makeshift raft. Rain mixed with leaves, branches, and broken bits of wood batter your head. From the water, you fish out a large piece of debris and use it to cover your head.

Then you hear a cry. "Help!"

Through the sheets of rain, you see a young woman flailing in the water. She yells again before she slips under the water.

Your raft is small. If you pull her onto it, you might both drown.

> To take a risk and help the young woman, turn to page 89.
>
> To ignore the woman's pleas, turn to page 92.

You launch yourself into the water and swim toward the broken roof. But it's farther away than it looked. Your soaked uniform is weighing you down. Finally, you grasp the edge of the roof and wriggle onto it.

The wreckage isn't only in the water. The howling wind hurls broken glass, boards, tree branches, and broken furniture through the air. You suddenly feel something hit your neck, and you lose consciousness. You never wake up again.

THE END

To follow another path, turn to page 9.
To learn more about the hurricane, turn to page 101.

The woman's head emerges from the water. She gasps for breath.

You lean over as far as you can and reach for her. "Grab my hand!" you shout.

Your hands touch, and you pull her with one arm, holding tightly to the raft with the other. She pulls herself onto the raft, and for a second it bobs in the water under her weight. But then the raft rights itself and keeps floating.

Suddenly, the raft slams against something solid. You're jolted and almost slide off, but the woman grabs your arm and holds you steady. "Look!" she says, pointing up.

You look up to see a tall, sturdy tree above you. The tree looks like it's stood for hundreds of years. You're sure it has weathered many storms.

Turn the page.

The woman has already hoisted herself to the lowest branch and is reaching for another.

You climb after her and find a sturdy branch. Then you hold on. The storm roars, too loud for you to talk.

The water rises and the wind howls, but the tree stays sturdy. When the storm finally wanes, you're drenched and cold, but alive. You and the woman, named Rachel, talk all night.

At daybreak, you and Rachel climb down. The tree is the only thing left standing as far as you can see. The entire city has been overturned and flattened.

You and Rachel make your way to City Hall, where people are gathering to find their loved ones. You don't want to say goodbye to her, so you don't. You make plans to meet.

When you and Rachel get married a few months later, you decide to stay in Galveston. Even though the city is destroyed, you help to rebuild it and make your home there for many years to come.

THE END

To follow another path, turn to page 9.
To learn more about the hurricane, turn to page 101.

You can't risk both of you drowning. You try to block out the woman's cries as you spin past her. You hope she survives.

Your raft lodges against a pile of debris. At dawn, you climb down and head for City Hall. Galveston doesn't look like the same city anymore. Mountains of rubble lie where buildings used to be.

City Hall is still standing, though. Chief Ketchum sends you and a team of officers to search for survivors. You scour the city, pulling wounded from the wreckage.

Then you hear a shout. One of your fellow officers is bending over a young woman. She sits up, holding a hand to her wounded head. Then she points at you. "That's him!" she shouts.

It's the woman you didn't help earlier. You're happy to see she survived.

"That officer did nothing to help me!" she cries, still pointing at you.

The other officers stare at you. You hang your head in shame. You failed in your duty to protect and serve.

THE END

To follow another path, turn to page 9.
To learn more about the hurricane, turn to page 101.

"We can try," you tell her. The woman sits back down.

You snap the reins. "Hyah!" you command.

The horses plunge forward through the water. But the rain has made the reins slippery, and the wind whips them from your hands, causing the horses to rear up. The wagon suddenly spins sideways and begins to tip.

The woman slides from the wagon into the water. She grabs a nearby tree and shouts at you to jump from the out-of-control wagon. But it's too late for you. The wagon overturns, and you're trapped beneath it. There's no escape from your watery grave.

THE END

To follow another path, turn to page 9.
To learn more about the hurricane, turn to page 101.

"No," the woman snaps. "I won't wait." Before you can stop her, she jumps from the wagon and disappears into the storm. You never see her again.

Soon a family waves you down, struggling through the storm. You help the children and parents into the wagon and take them to safety. You feel proud for helping the family. But you wish you could have done more.

By the next day, more than 8,000 people are dead. The city is destroyed, and countless bodies lie among the wreckage. There are too many bodies to bury on the island. They'll have to be buried at sea.

For your next duty, Police Chief Ketchum gives you two options. You can either help carry bodies to the waterfront, where they will be carried out into the gulf. Or you can patrol the city for looters.

To carry bodies, turn to page 96.
To patrol the city, turn to page 98.

There were too many storm victims to bury them normally. People gathered bodies to be buried at sea or burned.

Over the next few days, you carry body after body onto boats. The boats carry the dead out to sea. But then another horror happens. The bodies wash back to shore. They'll have to be burned instead.

Luckily, the police chief doesn't assign you that task. Instead, you help the Red Cross hand out food and supplies to those in need. You also help raise tents for the newly homeless to live in.

Although the destruction of the city is horrible, you find happiness in helping others. In 1902, construction begins on a seawall to protect the city from flooding. The city slowly comes back to life. You continue your duties as a police officer, keeping the people of Galveston safe.

THE END

To follow another path, turn to page 9.
To learn more about the hurricane, turn to page 101.

With the city destroyed, many people began looting wrecked buildings and dead bodies to find a way to survive.

On foot, you patrol the destroyed city. The morning sun shines down, and the sky is nearly cloudless. The calm weather seems unbelievable after the rages of last night's storm.

You come across a group of boys sifting through the wreckage for valuables. As you haul them to jail, you feel sorry for them. They lost everything. Maybe they're just trying to survive.

By the end of the day, you've caught a dozen looters. You know that looting is wrong, but you don't feel right about sending people to jail after such a horrific event. You know there must be other ways to help.

You make a big decision. You resign from the police force. Then you set up a free service to help people reunite with their loved ones. With your investigative skills and knowledge of the city, you're good at your new role. Many stories end in sorrow. But with your help, other people's stories can have a happy ending.

THE END

To follow another path, turn to page 9.
To learn more about the hurricane, turn to page 101.

Few buildings were left standing in Galveston after the powerful hurricane hit the city.

CHAPTER 5
STORM OF THE CENTURY

The Great Galveston Hurricane swept over Galveston, Texas, on the afternoon of September 8, 1900. The storm killed between 8,000 and 12,000 people. It is the deadliest natural disaster in United States history.

At its height, experts believe the hurricane whipped up winds of 140 miles (225 kilometers) per hour. Today, it would be classified as a Category 4 hurricane by the Saffir-Simpson scale. More than 3,600 buildings and homes were destroyed. The storm surge caused 15 feet (4.6 meters) of water to flood the city. Many people drowned. Others were killed under collapsed buildings or by flying objects. Some were carried away into the Gulf of Mexico.

SAFFIR-SIMPSON SCALE

CATEGORY	WIND SPEED
5	156+ miles (251 km) per hour
4	131–155 mph (210–249 kph)
3	111–130 mph (179–209 kph)
2	96–110 mph (155–177 kph)
1	74–95 mph (119–153 kph)
Tropical Storm	39–73 mph (63–117.5 kph)
Tropical Depression	0–38 mph (0–61 kph)

When the storm ended in the early hours of September 9, Galveston was almost destroyed. Thousands had lost their homes. Survivors had no food or water. City officials set up rescue teams to search for survivors and food. No one knew when help would arrive from the mainland. Telegraph and telephone lines had gone down in the storm.

On September 15, the Red Cross arrived. They set up tents for the homeless and handed out food and supplies. There were too many dead bodies to bury. Instead, bodies had to be dumped into the sea or burned in funeral pyres along the shore.

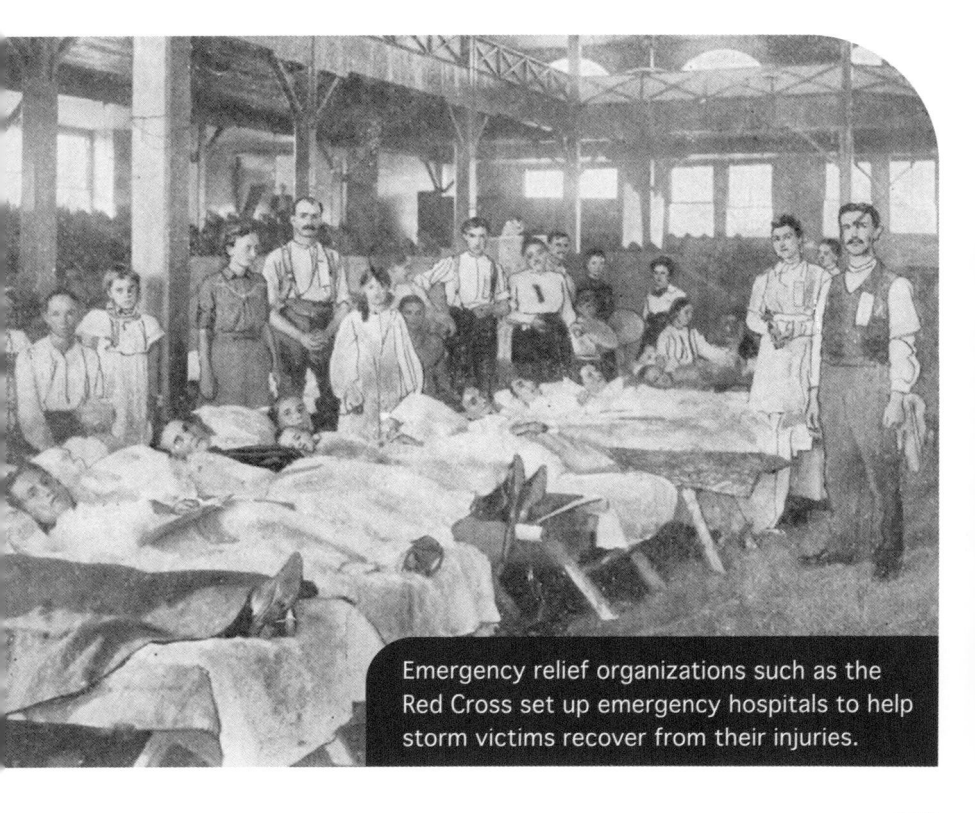

Emergency relief organizations such as the Red Cross set up emergency hospitals to help storm victims recover from their injuries.

In 1900 Galveston had a diverse population. Many white, Black, and Latino men worked together on the busy waterfront. But the city was also segregated. White people and people of color lived in separate neighborhoods and attended separate schools.

When the hurricane hit, people of all races helped save each other. A Black man named Daniel Ransom saved 45 people by diving into the water and pulling them to safety. Both Black and white people huddled together in homes and buildings.

But after the hurricane, racism reared its ugly head. Black men were forced to carry away the dead. Black people were often singled out and accused of looting as well.

> A 17-foot (5.2-m) seawall was built next to the shoreline to help protect Galveston from future storms. It was completed in 1904.

The destruction of Galveston led to advances in weather forecasting. After the hurricane, more efforts were put into studying and predicting hurricanes. Today the National Weather Service tracks storms and weather patterns around the clock. The service issues many weather watches and warnings so people can be prepared when severe weather strikes.

MOST DESTRUCTIVE HURRICANES IN U.S. HISTORY

LAKE OKEECHOBEE HURRICANE
The Lake Okeechobee Hurricane struck South Florida in 1928, claiming 2,500 lives in South Florida and more than 4,000 lives total. The hurricane caused the water of Lake Okeechobee to surge and flood surrounding farmland, drowning thousands of people. The damage was $100 million ($1.6 billion today).

GREAT NEW ENGLAND HURRICANE
The Great New England Hurricane of 1938 caused 600 to 800 deaths and more than $300 million ($5.7 billion today) in damage. The storm arrived without warning. Weather forecasters predicted the storm would head out to sea, but instead it hit New England, striking Connecticut, Rhode Island, and Massachusetts. The hurricane weakened as it moved upward to Canada.

HURRICANE ANDREW
Hurricane Andrew struck the Bahamas, South Florida, and South Louisiana in 1992. The storm caused $26.5 billion in damage ($50.8 billion today). Sixty five people died.

HURRICANE KATRINA

In August 2005, Hurricane Katrina made landfall in southern Louisiana. The City of New Orleans suffered a great deal of damage. The storm claimed 1,836 lives and caused $81 billion in damage.

HURRICANE SANDY

In 2012, Hurricane Sandy swept over eight countries. It killed 75 people in the Caribbean and nearly 150 people in the United States. Sandy caused the most damage in the states of New York and New Jersey. Maryland, Delaware, Connecticut, Massachusetts, and Rhode Island were also damaged.

HURRICANE MARIA

In September 2017, Hurricane Maria devastated the northern Caribbean, causing more than 3,000 deaths. The U.S. Territory of Puerto Rico sustained much damage, suffering from flooding, power outages, and lack of resources. Hurricane Maria caused $91.61 billion in damage.

OTHER PATHS TO EXPLORE

>>> Galveston was a major shipping port. Many sailors were aboard cargo ships and barges when the storm struck. What would it be like to be on a ship in the Gulf of Mexico during the hurricane? What would sailors need to do to survive the storm?

>>> With its beaches and waterfront views, Galveston was a popular vacation spot. Many tourists were in Galveston when the hurricane hit. What would it be like to be a tourist in a strange city when a disastrous hurricane strikes? How would you know where to go to find help?

>>> In the wake of the hurricane, the Red Cross arrived in Galveston. The volunteers delivered food and supplies and tended to the wounded. Imagine you were a Red Cross volunteer after the Galveston Hurricane. What do you think the experience would be like to help the survivors?

BIBLIOGRAPHY

Bixel, Patricia Bellis, and Elizabeth Hayes Turner. *Galveston and the 1900 Storm: Catastrophe and Catalyst.* Austin, TX: University of Texas Press, 2000.

Eyewitness to History: The Galveston Hurricane of 1900. eyewitnesstohistory.com/galveston.htm

The History Channel: How the Galveston Hurricane of 1900 Became the Deadliest U.S. Natural Disaster. history.com/news/how-the-galveston-hurricane-of-1900-became-the-deadliest-u-s-natural-disaster

Larson, Erik. *Isaac's Storm: A Man, A Time, and the Deadliest Hurricane in History.* New York: Crown Publishers, 1999.

National Oceanic and Atmospheric Administration: The Great Galveston Hurricane of 1900. celebrating200years.noaa.gov/magazine/galv_hurricane/welcome.html

Roker, Al. *The Storm of the Century: Tragedy, Heroism, Survival, and the Epic True Story of America's Deadliest Natural Disaster.* New York: HarperCollins Publishers, 2015.

Texas State Historical Association: Galveston Hurricane of 1900. tshaonline.org/handbook/entries/galveston-hurricane-of-1900

GLOSSARY

altocumulus clouds (al-toh-KYOO-myuh-luhs KLOWDZ)—clouds made up of rounded clumps that are organized in layers or rolls

amateur (AH-muh-chuhr)—someone who is inexperienced or unskilled in a certain activity

causeway (KAWZ-way)—a raised road or path, usually across water

cyclone (SY-klohn)—a storm with strong winds that rotates around a center of low atmospheric pressure and brings heavy rain

debris (duh-BREE)—the scattered pieces of something that has been broken or destroyed

evacuate (i-VA-kyuh-wayt)—to leave an area during a time of danger

kerosene (KER-uh-seen)—a thin, colorless fuel made from petroleum

meteorologist (mee-tee-uh-RAW-luh-jist)—a scientist who studies and predicts the weather

promotion (pruh-MOH-shuhn)—a better or higher paying job with more authority and responsibility

pyre (PYER)—a pile of wood built to burn a dead body

segregated (SEH-gruh-gay-tuhd)—separated by race

READ MORE

Gunderson, Jessica. *Carrie and the Great Storm.* North Mankato, MN: Capstone Press, 2019.

Hubbard, Ben. *Hurricanes and Tornadoes.* Danbury, CT: Franklin Watts Publishing, 2019.

Tarshis, Lauren. *I Survived the Galveston Hurricane, 1900.* New York: Scholastic Inc., 2021.

INTERNET SITES

1900 Galveston Hurricane
history.com/topics/natural-disasters-and-environment/1900-galveston-hurricane

Galveston Hurricane of 1900
kids.britannica.com/students/article/Galveston-hurricane-of-1900/623413

Galveston Hurricane of 1900
nps.gov/articles/galveston-hurricane-of-1900.htm

ABOUT THE AUTHOR

Jessica Gunderson grew up in the small town of Washburn, North Dakota. She has a bachelor's degree from the University of North Dakota and an MFA in Creative Writing from Minnesota State University, Mankato. She has written more than 75 books for young readers. Her book *President Lincoln's Killer and the America He Left Behind* won a 2018 Eureka! Nonfiction Children's Book Silver Award. She currently lives in Madison, Wisconsin, with her husband and three cats.

Photo Credits
Alamy: CPA Media Pte Ltd, 35, Everett Collection Inc, 55, Niday Picture Library, 36, 103, Science History Images, 96, 100; Associated Press: Sisters of Charity, (house) Cover; Getty Images: Historical, 6, Library of Congress, 61, Paul Popper/Popperfoto, 10, Sepia Times, 46, Universal History Archive, 21, 70; Library of Congress, 73, 82, 98, 105; Shutterstock: Mikhail hoboton Popov, 66, Mimadeo, 42, ro9drigo, (sky) design element, Cover